Laurie Parker

HIDDEN PICTURE

# GARDEN
## ALPHABET

WRITTEN AND ILLUSTRATED BY
## LAURIE PARKER

ACKNOWLEDGMENT:

Thanks to Cyndi Clark as always!

## Note to Gardeners from the Author:

If I didn't have to work, I would garden all day and create art all night! In the minimal spare time I do have, I work in my yard as much as possible. So know that as a gardener myself, I am totally aware that many, if not all, of my illustrations show the blooming at once of several flowers, some of which do not bloom at the same time (i.e. daffodils/ daisies, rhododendrons/rudbeckia). Shade and full-sun plants are depicted side by side in some scenes. This is simply due to the fun ABC format of the book, which obviously groups certain words together in the verses. The artwork accompanies the text, and therefore I had to take liberties in the illustrations. They are designed to represent a cer- tain letter of the alphabet and to include the things mentioned for that letter in the poet- ry. This is a book meant to introduce children to gardening concepts, and I tried to mix in enough whimsy to make it captivating. And most of that whimsy is in the artwork. Anyway, wouldn't a garden where everything bloomed at once be truly magical!?

Printed and bound in South Korea by Pacifica Communications.
9  8  7  6  5  4  3  2  1

*For my sister Lynn*

Come into the garden. There's so much to see!
Come learn lots of marvelous things…A to Z!

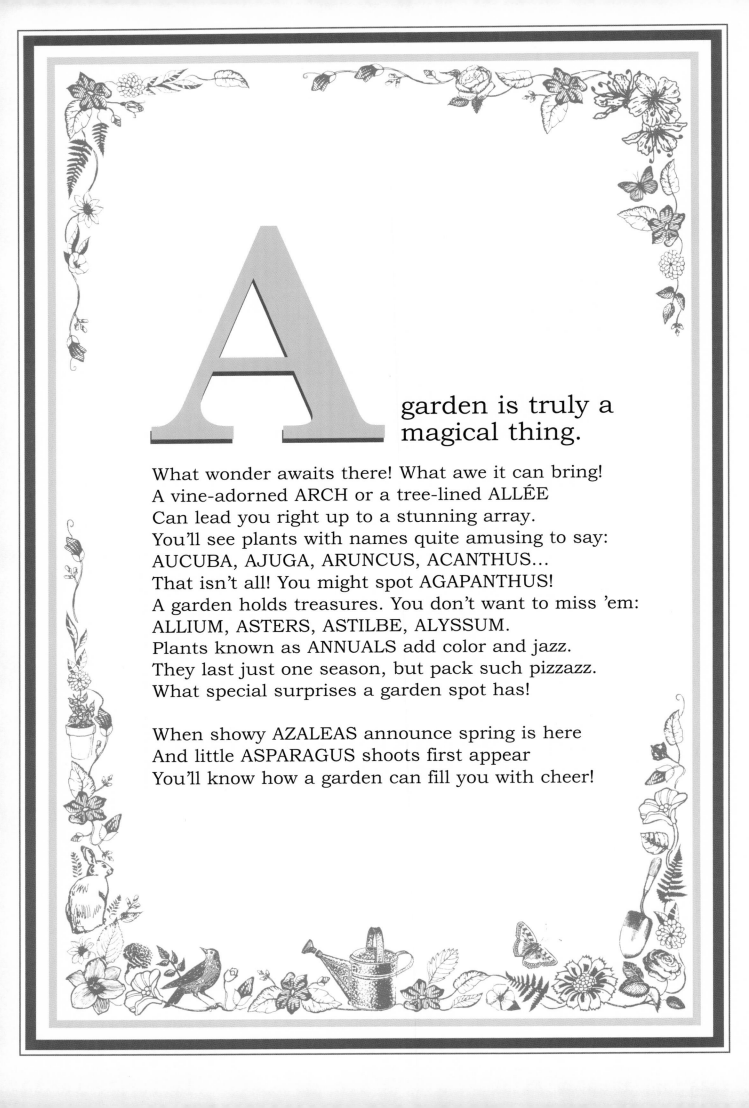

# A

garden is truly a magical thing.

What wonder awaits there! What awe it can bring!
A vine-adorned ARCH or a tree-lined ALLÉE
Can lead you right up to a stunning array.
You'll see plants with names quite amusing to say:
AUCUBA, AJUGA, ARUNCUS, ACANTHUS…
That isn't all! You might spot AGAPANTHUS!
A garden holds treasures. You don't want to miss 'em:
ALLIUM, ASTERS, ASTILBE, ALYSSUM.
Plants known as ANNUALS add color and jazz.
They last just one season, but pack such pizzazz.
What special surprises a garden spot has!

When showy AZALEAS announce spring is here
And little ASPARAGUS shoots first appear
You'll know how a garden can fill you with cheer!

A garden's the type of place ANGELS might hide.
This garden has three angel statues inside
And three that are hidden can also be spied!

# B

eing a gardener
brings blessings
and joys.

It's something that benefits both girls AND boys.
A boring backyard can become something grand.
What can you put there so it isn't bland?
BOTTLE TREES. BIRDBATHS.
BEDS edged with old brick.
BLUEBERRY BUSHES. Some BASIL to pick.
BORDERS of flowers that sound so bizarre:
BUGBANE and BEARDTONGUE beside
BLAZING STAR.
Along with BEGONIAS and BEE BALM you'll need
BACHELOR'S BUTTONS and BUTTERFLY WEED,
Beautiful BOXWOOD shaped into a ball
And a BENCH where you'll sit just beholding it all!

BEES *are like buddies for gardens, no doubt.*
*They pollinate flowers. That helps the plants out.*
*Can you find nine busy bees buzzing about?*

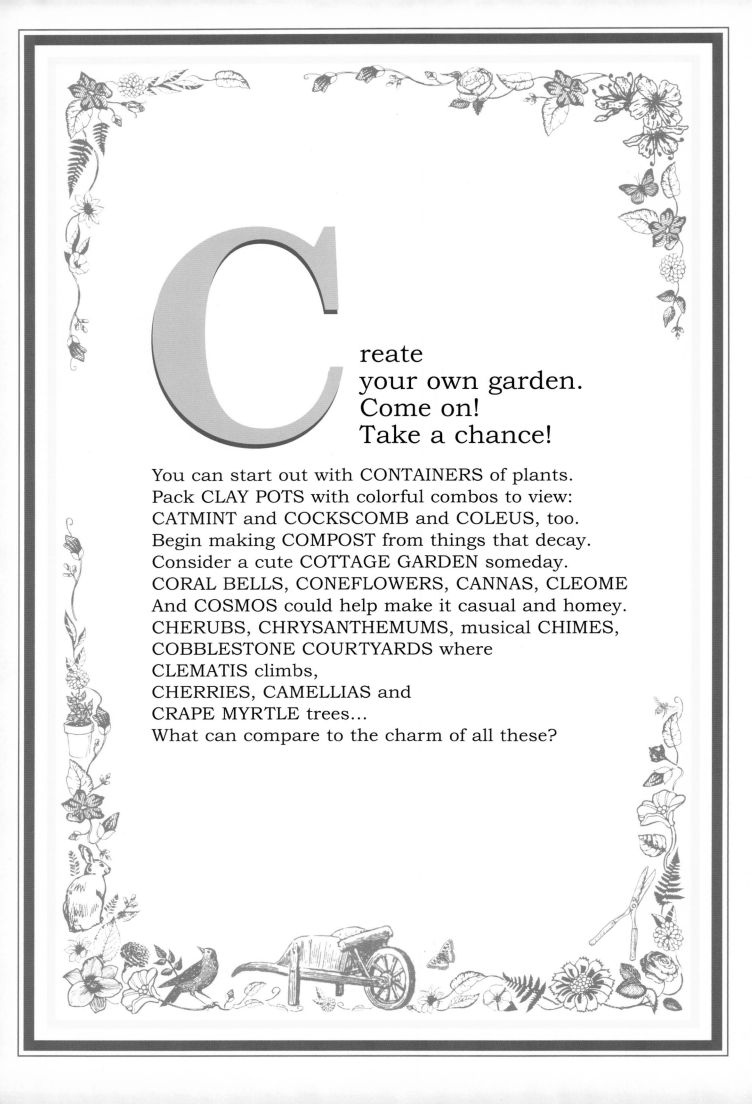

# C

reate
your own garden.
Come on!
Take a chance!

You can start out with CONTAINERS of plants.
Pack CLAY POTS with colorful combos to view:
CATMINT and COCKSCOMB and COLEUS, too.
Begin making COMPOST from things that decay.
Consider a cute COTTAGE GARDEN someday.
CORAL BELLS, CONEFLOWERS, CANNAS, CLEOME
And COSMOS could help make it casual and homey.
CHERUBS, CHRYSANTHEMUMS, musical CHIMES,
COBBLESTONE COURTYARDS where
CLEMATIS climbs,
CHERRIES, CAMELLIAS and
CRAPE MYRTLE trees...
What can compare to the charm of all these?

*This yard has three CARDINALS, or redbirds. Find these.*
*Then search for two other birds called CHICKADEES.*
*Four CATS are here looking for birds they can seize.*

# D

igging in dirt
with your hands
is divine...

And gardening allows you to dream and design.
There's not a dull moment. There's plenty to do—
Like DEADHEADING flowers with
Blooms that are through.
Plants that have spread out in clumps need
DIVIDING.
What to plant where?
There's a lot of deciding!
DECIDUOUS trees drop their leaves in the fall
And some will work diligently raking them all.
The diehard pull DANDELIONS up one by one.
A gardener's duties are never quite done.
But, oh, the delight when DELPHINIUMS grow
And DOGWOODS and DAFFODILS dance to and fro.
DAYLILIES, DAHLIAS and DAISIES galore...
It's a dazzling display that will make your heart soar!

DRAGONFLIES *really are spellbinding things.*
*They dart through the air on such delicate wings.*
*They'll drop by quite often if water is near.*
*Can you detect five in the garden shown here?*

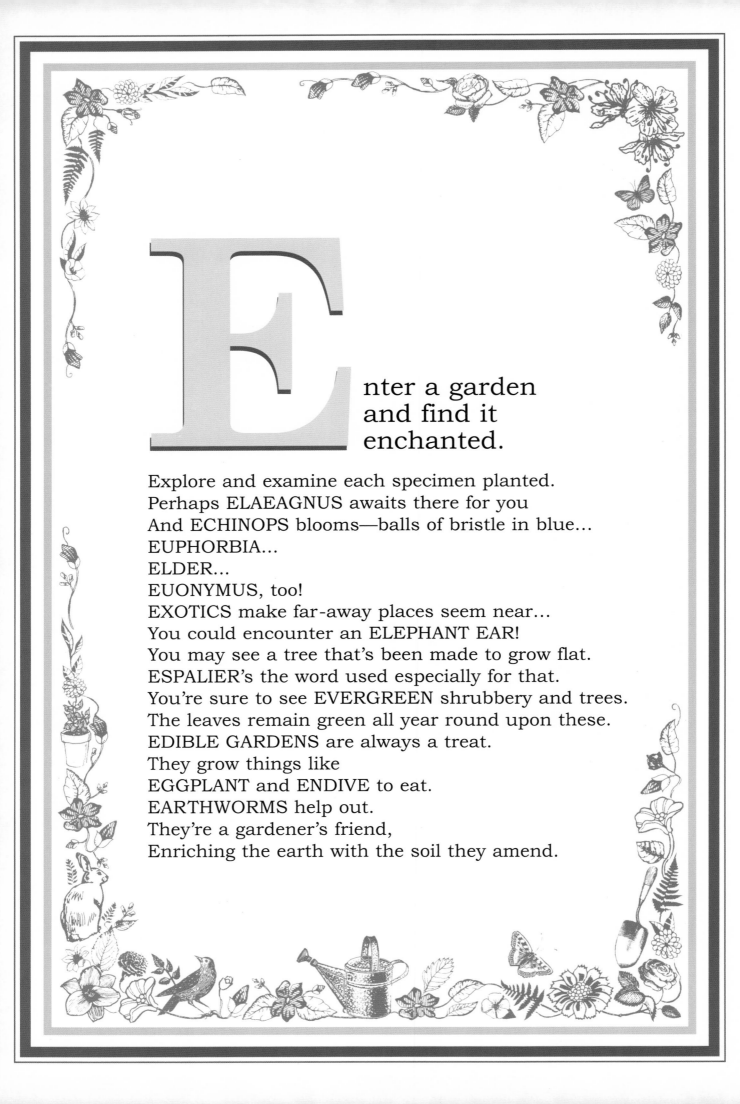

# Enter a garden and find it enchanted.

Explore and examine each specimen planted.
Perhaps ELAEAGNUS awaits there for you
And ECHINOPS blooms—balls of bristle in blue...
EUPHORBIA...
ELDER...
EUONYMUS, too!
EXOTICS make far-away places seem near...
You could encounter an ELEPHANT EAR!
You may see a tree that's been made to grow flat.
ESPALIER's the word used especially for that.
You're sure to see EVERGREEN shrubbery and trees.
The leaves remain green all year round upon these.
EDIBLE GARDENS are always a treat.
They grow things like
EGGPLANT and ENDIVE to eat.
EARTHWORMS help out.
They're a gardener's friend,
Enriching the earth with the soil they amend.

*An EASTER EGG hunt among flowers is fun.*
*Eight eggs are concealed here. Try finding each one!*

# F

OXGLOVE,
FORGET-ME-NOTS,
FEVERFEW,
FLAX...

FLOWERS have fantastic forms and fun facts!
With feathery FOLIAGE that's known as a FROND,
FERNS are a plant of which gardeners are fond.
Follow a curved FLAGSTONE path if you wish.
You might find a pond full of glimmering FISH
Or a fabulous FOUNTAIN that gurgles and flows
Or a FRUIT TREE like FIG or a small FAIRY ROSE.
Some gardens are FORMAL, configured in line.
But most are plain folksy, and that is just fine!

*Outside is where fantasy lets you insist*
*That FROGS become princes and FAIRIES exist.*
*Five frogs and five fairies here shouldn't be missed!*

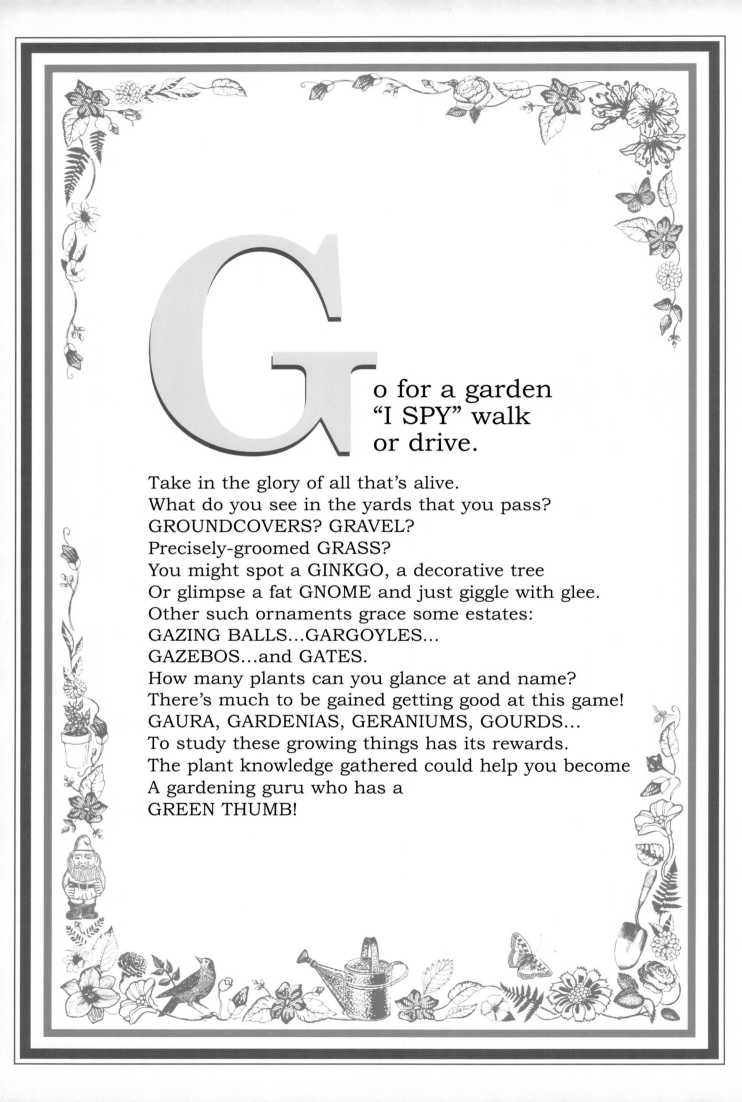

# G

o for a garden
"I SPY" walk
or drive.

Take in the glory of all that's alive.
What do you see in the yards that you pass?
GROUNDCOVERS? GRAVEL?
Precisely-groomed GRASS?
You might spot a GINKGO, a decorative tree
Or glimpse a fat GNOME and just giggle with glee.
Other such ornaments grace some estates:
GAZING BALLS...GARGOYLES...
GAZEBOS...and GATES.
How many plants can you glance at and name?
There's much to be gained getting good at this game!
GAURA, GARDENIAS, GERANIUMS, GOURDS...
To study these growing things has its rewards.
The plant knowledge gathered could help you become
A gardening guru who has a
GREEN THUMB!

GARDEN GLOVES help. They protect hands from wear.
Someone here lost one that went with a pair.
Look for the glove…and five GNOMES here and there.

# H

ow happy
you'll feel
in a haven
outside

Where HOLLY and HEDGES form places to hide.
Head out of the house! There is heavenly weather
And HOLLYHOCKS, HOSTAS,
HIBISCUS and HEATHER,
Huge French HYDRANGEAS and HELIOTROPE.
You'll tell them hello very soon they all hope!
Harvest HERBS. Hug a tree.
Watch a HUMMINGBIRD FEEDER.
Hang out in a HAMMOCK. Your life will be sweeter!
Gardening's a hobby you'll never outgrow,
So say, "Hallelujah," and go grab a HOE!

*The feeder's where three hungry HUMMINGBIRDS hover.*
*Four others are elsewhere to hunt and discover.*

# I

magine a garden
infused with
perfume...

You see ICEBERG ROSES in cascades of bloom.
IMPATIENS are nestled 'neath IVY-draped oaks.
There's a storybook feeling their color evokes.
An old IRONWORK gate with an intricate door
Invites you beyond to investigate more.
The other side beckons. What waits there ahead?
INDIAN BLANKETS with bands of bright red?
Or IRISES maybe? What do you foresee?
That's how intriguing a garden can be!

*Dragonflies, butterflies, bees, beetles, ants...*
*They're INSECTS. They all have six legs used to prance.*
*Many insects are found in this scene. Take a glance!*
*How many can you count? Inspect all the plants!*

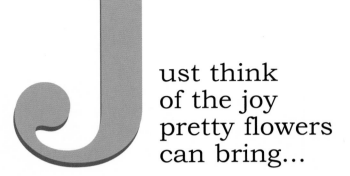

# J

ust think
of the joy
pretty flowers
can bring...

Like JACK-IN-THE-PULPIT or JONQUILS in spring.
Wee JOHNNY JUMP-UPS...unique JACOB'S LADDER...
They're like living jewels that make your heart gladder.
The fragrance of JASMINE, a JUNIPER tree
Or JAPANESE MAPLE can cause jubilee.
Keeping a gardening JOURNAL is fun.
Jot down what bloomed when and how plants have done.

# K

nowledge is key
in keen gardeners'
minds.

They keep up with facts. They have plans of all kinds.
A KNOT GARDEN's seemingly knitted detail...
Delectable greens like KOHLRABI and KALE...
Potagers, quaint KITCHEN GARDENS in France...
New KNOCKOUT ROSES for added romance...
Living kaleidoscopes made out of plants...
Gardeners daydream of things such as these
When they're working hard, kneeling down on their knees.

The birds known as JAYS make a loud, noisy cry.
They're kin to the crow, so perhaps that is why.
Blue jays are common birds. Look! There are three!
A fourth is nearby somewhere. Where can he be?

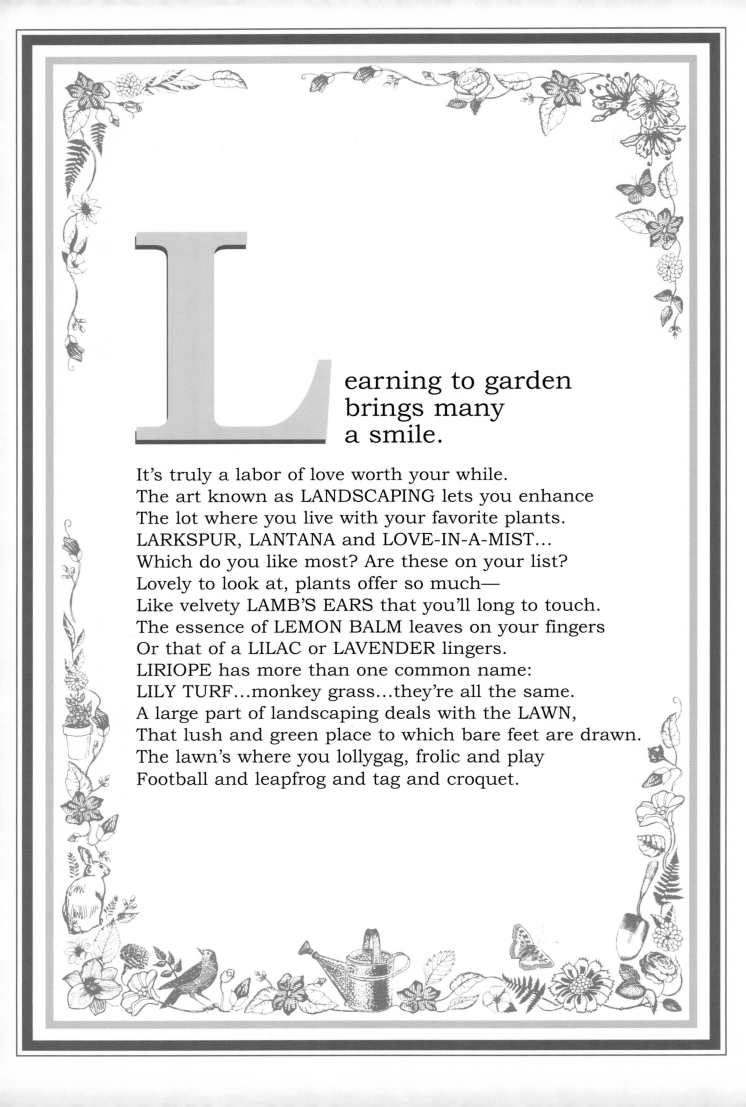

# L

earning to garden
brings many
a smile.

It's truly a labor of love worth your while.
The art known as LANDSCAPING lets you enhance
The lot where you live with your favorite plants.
LARKSPUR, LANTANA and LOVE-IN-A-MIST...
Which do you like most? Are these on your list?
Lovely to look at, plants offer so much—
Like velvety LAMB'S EARS that you'll long to touch.
The essence of LEMON BALM leaves on your fingers
Or that of a LILAC or LAVENDER lingers.
LIRIOPE has more than one common name:
LILY TURF...monkey grass...they're all the same.
A large part of landscaping deals with the LAWN,
That lush and green place to which bare feet are drawn.
The lawn's where you lollygag, frolic and play
Football and leapfrog and tag and croquet.

*Gardeners love LADYBUGS. Do you know why?*
*They eat tiny insects that could make plants die.*
*Locating eight here requires a good eye!*

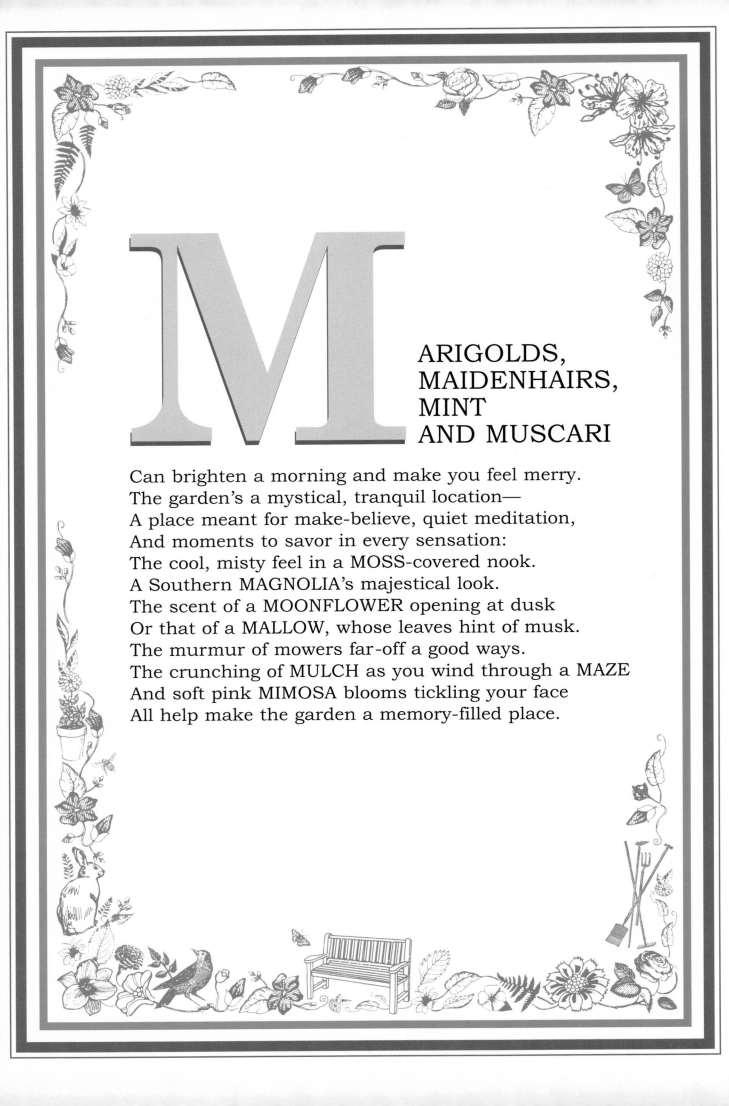

# M

ARIGOLDS,
MAIDENHAIRS,
MINT
AND MUSCARI

Can brighten a morning and make you feel merry.
The garden's a mystical, tranquil location—
A place meant for make-believe, quiet meditation,
And moments to savor in every sensation:
The cool, misty feel in a MOSS-covered nook.
A Southern MAGNOLIA's majestical look.
The scent of a MOONFLOWER opening at dusk
Or that of a MALLOW, whose leaves hint of musk.
The murmur of mowers far-off a good ways.
The crunching of MULCH as you wind through a MAZE
And soft pink MIMOSA blooms tickling your face
All help make the garden a memory-filled place.

*One big MONARCH butterfly likes the MONARDA.*
*Finding ten more just might be a bit harder...*

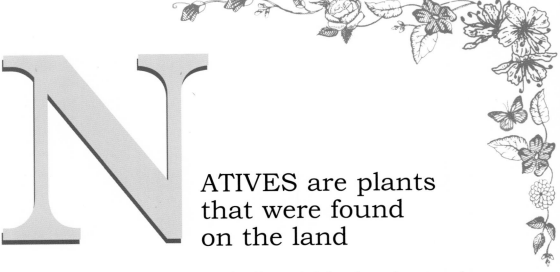

# N

ATIVES are plants
that were found
on the land

Where now all the newly-built neighborhoods stand.
A NURSERY is where many plants are controlled.
They're grown there and nurtured so they can be sold.
NANDINA is common in yards—front and center.
You'll notice the nice bright red berries in winter.
Take note of yards near you. You just never know
Exactly when pink NAKED LADIES will show!

# O

h, how sublime
to observe a
June day

Where OAKLEAF HYDRANGEAS and
OSTRICH FERNS sway.
It feels extra sweet when you call them your own
Because they are something you've cared for and grown.
One option for how it could all come to be
Is ORGANIC GARDENING. That's chemical-free!
ONIONS...OXALIS...whatever you raise,
It can be done without harsh, manmade sprays.

*A Baltimore ORIOLE bird has stopped by.*
*He's orange and black, so he's easy to spy.*
*He thinks that this OGEE arch makes a good perch.*
*You'll find one more oriole bird if you search...*

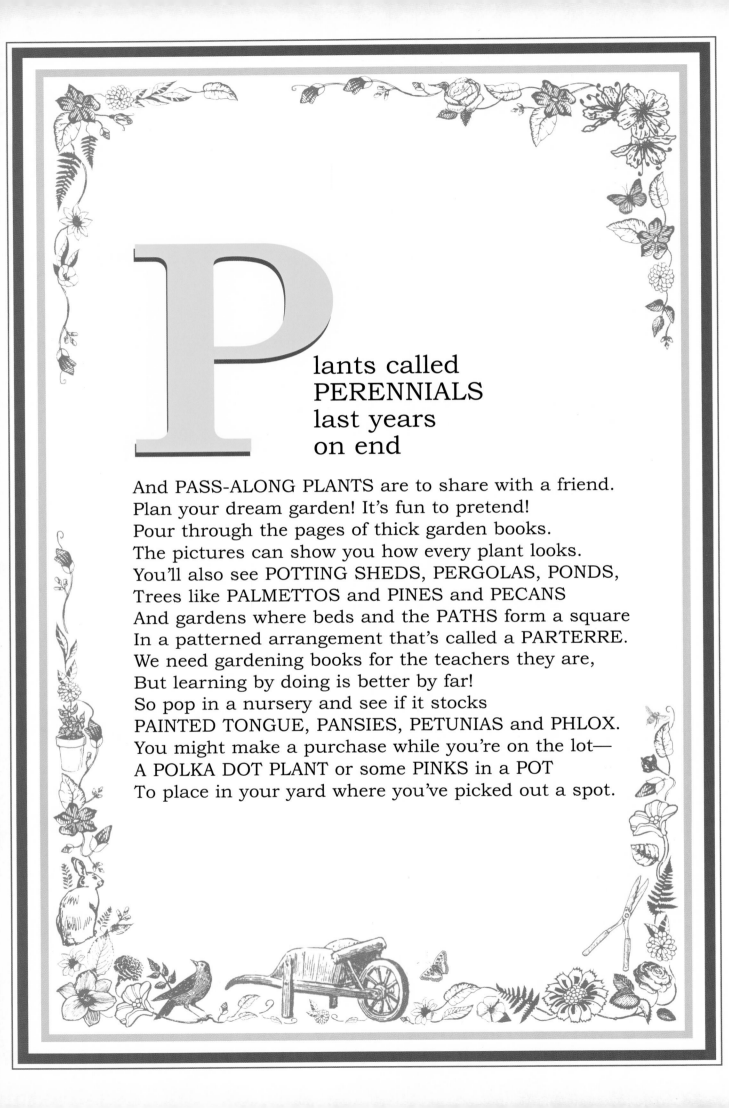

**P**lants called
PERENNIALS
last years
on end

And PASS-ALONG PLANTS are to share with a friend.
Plan your dream garden! It's fun to pretend!
Pour through the pages of thick garden books.
The pictures can show you how every plant looks.
You'll also see POTTING SHEDS, PERGOLAS, PONDS,
Trees like PALMETTOS and PINES and PECANS
And gardens where beds and the PATHS form a square
In a patterned arrangement that's called a PARTERRE.
We need gardening books for the teachers they are,
But learning by doing is better by far!
So pop in a nursery and see if it stocks
PAINTED TONGUE, PANSIES, PETUNIAS and PHLOX.
You might make a purchase while you're on the lot—
A POLKA DOT PLANT or some PINKS in a POT
To place in your yard where you've picked out a spot.

*PRUNING's like haircuts for shrubs and small trees.*
*Pruners are useful. All gardeners need these.*
*But someone misplaced a new pair in this yard.*
*Can you help to find them? Please search for them hard!*

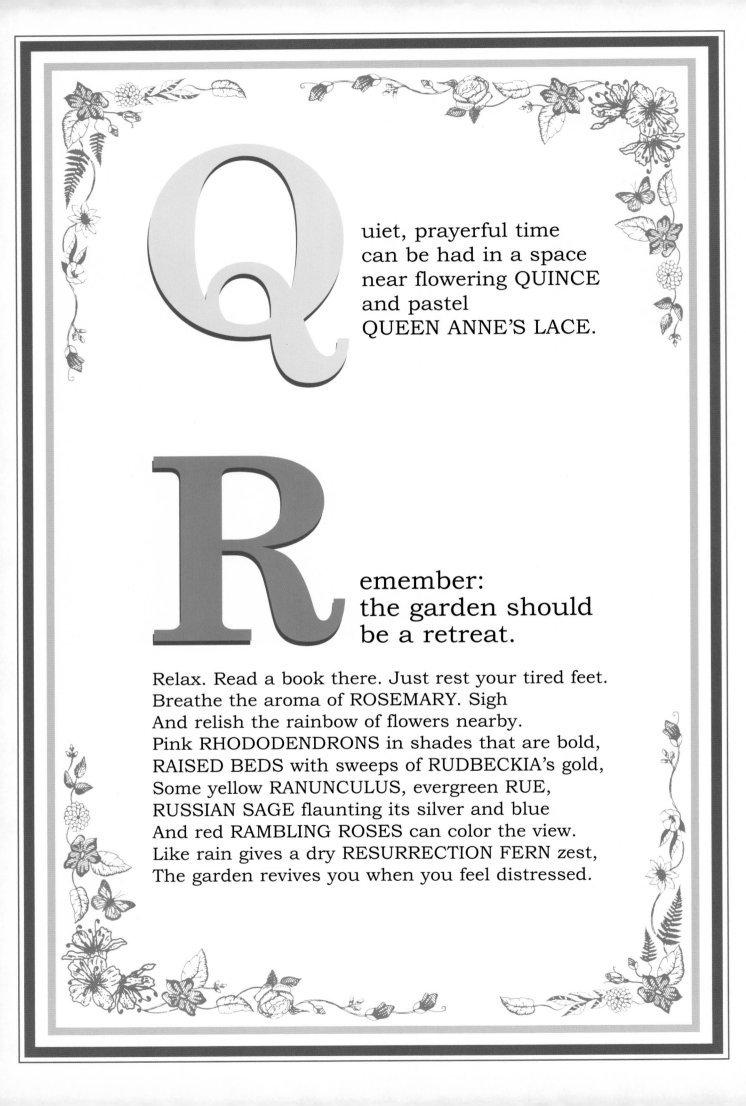

**Q**uiet, prayerful time
can be had in a space
near flowering QUINCE
and pastel
QUEEN ANNE'S LACE.

**R**emember:
the garden should
be a retreat.

Relax. Read a book there. Just rest your tired feet.
Breathe the aroma of ROSEMARY. Sigh
And relish the rainbow of flowers nearby.
Pink RHODODENDRONS in shades that are bold,
RAISED BEDS with sweeps of RUDBECKIA's gold,
Some yellow RANUNCULUS, evergreen RUE,
RUSSIAN SAGE flaunting its silver and blue
And red RAMBLING ROSES can color the view.
Like rain gives a dry RESURRECTION FERN zest,
The garden revives you when you feel distressed.

When gardeners dig or spray beds with a hose,
The earthworms start wriggling. And ROBINS love those!
This yard's full of robins. A bird rendezvous!
But one rascally robin is hiding from you!

**S**ome gardens are SECRET. Their mystery enthralls.

They're tucked out of sight behind
SHRUBS or STONE walls.
Designed for the sense of seclusion they bring,
They might hold a STATUE or even a SWING.
All gardens are special and good for the soul,
So go to one soon for a leisurely stroll.
STEPPING STONES usher you. Take it real slow
So you can enjoy the spectacular show.
SNAPDRAGONS, SPIDERWORT,
SEA HOLLIES, SEDGE,
SPRUCE, SNOW-IN-SUMMER, a SPIREA hedge,
SALVIA, STRAWBERRIES, SCUPPERNONG grapes,
STANDARDS in whimsical lollipop shapes
And big, smiling SUNFLOWERS showing their faces
Are part of a splendorous outside oasis.

*Search for four SUN FACES, one garden SPIDER,*
*One little SNAKE that's a real sneaky hider,*
*Six SWALLOWTAIL butterflies flitting, two SNAILS*
*And the shape of a SWAN that is in the details.*

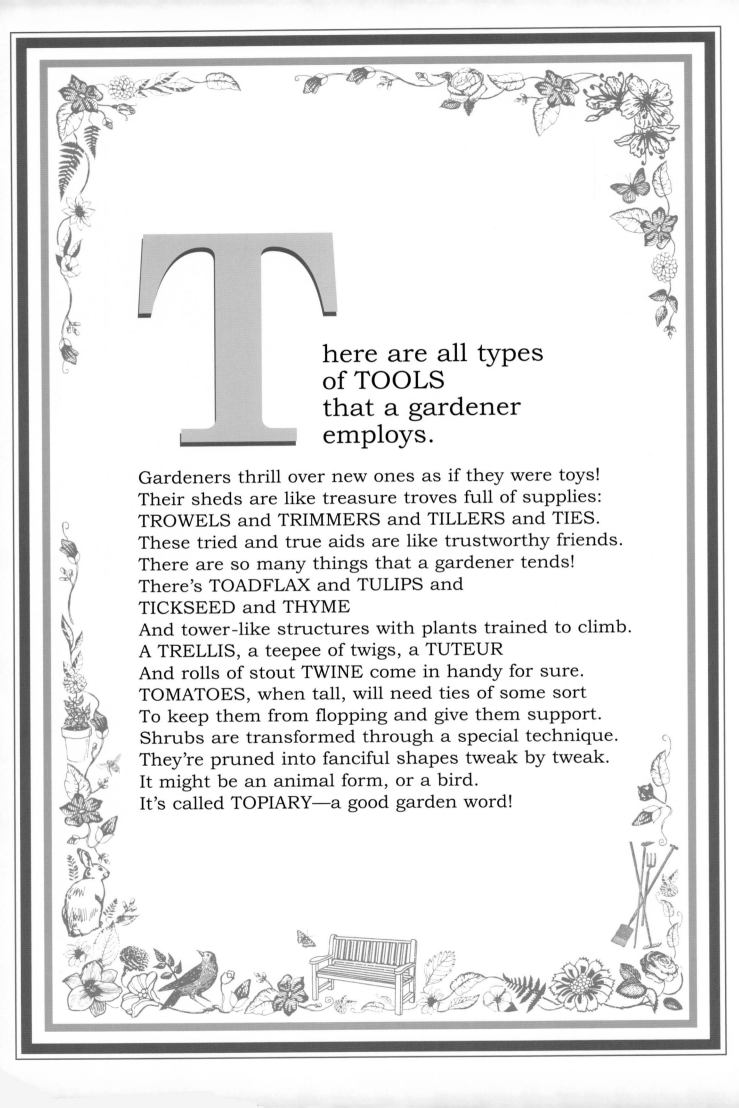

# T

here are all types
of TOOLS
that a gardener
employs.

Gardeners thrill over new ones as if they were toys!
Their sheds are like treasure troves full of supplies:
TROWELS and TRIMMERS and TILLERS and TIES.
These tried and true aids are like trustworthy friends.
There are so many things that a gardener tends!
There's TOADFLAX and TULIPS and
TICKSEED and THYME
And tower-like structures with plants trained to climb.
A TRELLIS, a teepee of twigs, a TUTEUR
And rolls of stout TWINE come in handy for sure.
TOMATOES, when tall, will need ties of some sort
To keep them from flopping and give them support.
Shrubs are transformed through a special technique.
They're pruned into fanciful shapes tweak by tweak.
It might be an animal form, or a bird.
It's called TOPIARY—a good garden word!

TOADS are terrific! Their tongues catch the bugs.
They eat many pests that are harmful—like slugs.
In this yard, a toadstool's where two toads abide.
They are not in there now. They are somewhere outside.

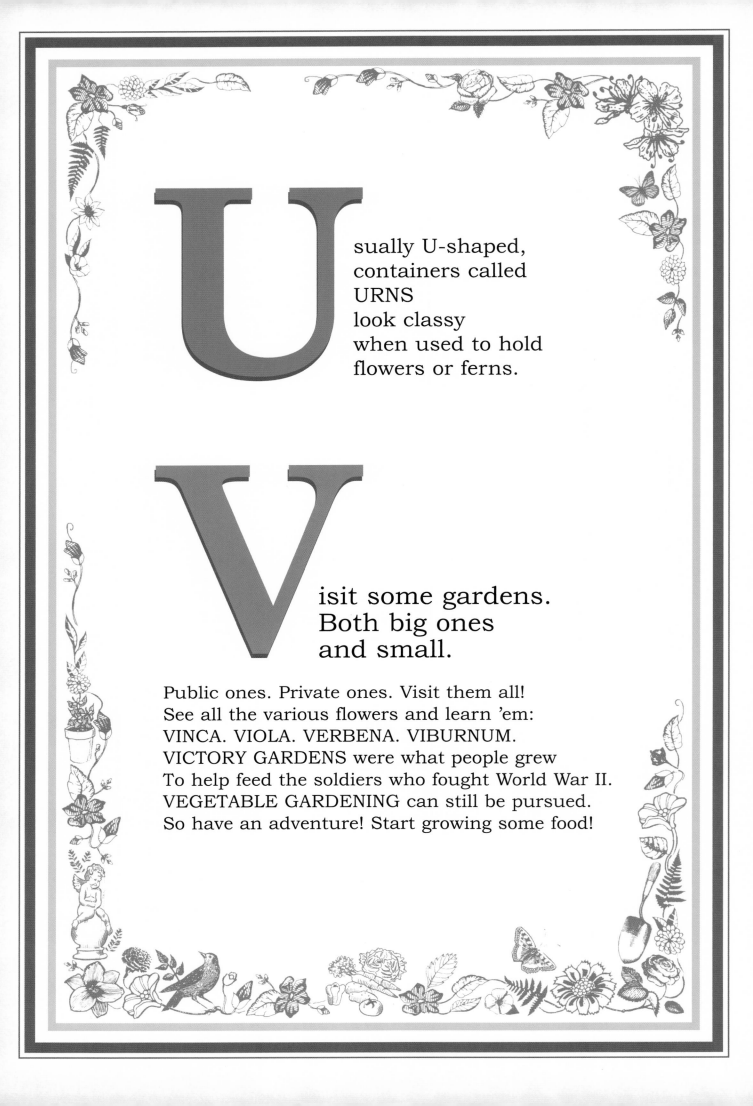

**U**sually U-shaped,
containers called
URNS
look classy
when used to hold
flowers or ferns.

**V**isit some gardens.
Both big ones
and small.

Public ones. Private ones. Visit them all!
See all the various flowers and learn 'em:
VINCA. VIOLA. VERBENA. VIBURNUM.
VICTORY GARDENS were what people grew
To help feed the soldiers who fought World War II.
VEGETABLE GARDENING can still be pursued.
So have an adventure! Start growing some food!

*The VICEROY butterfly fools folks a lot.*
*They think it's a monarch, but it's really not.*
*This garden has six viceroys you can spot.*

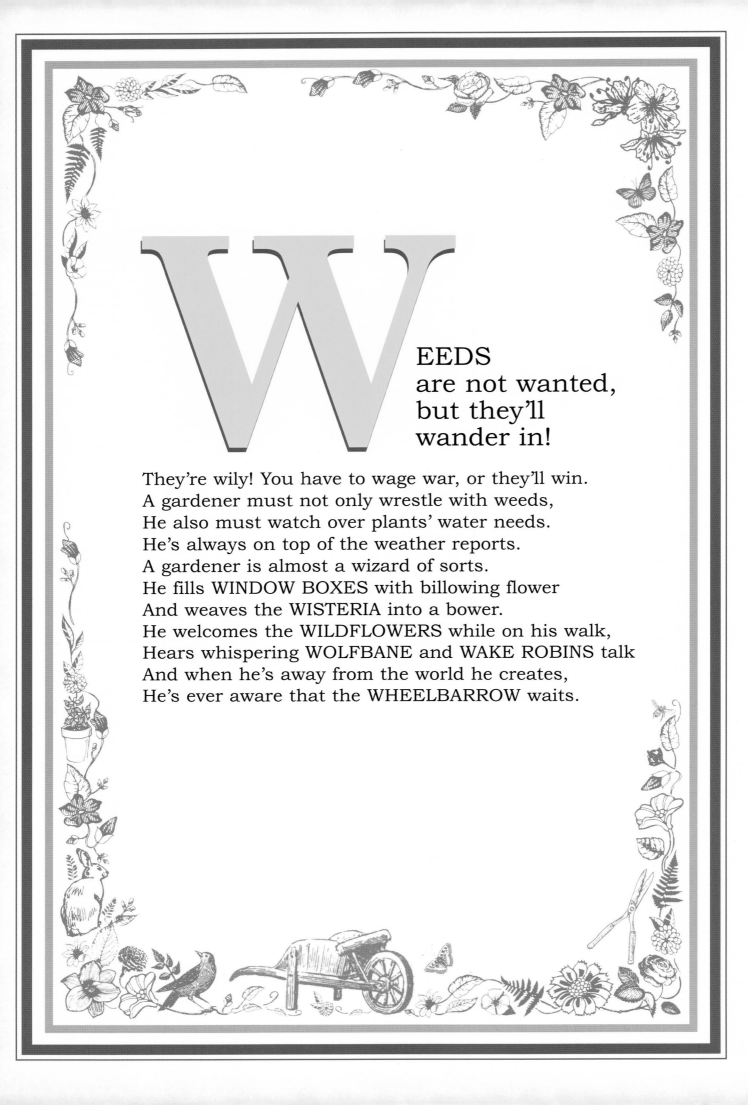

# W

EEDS
are not wanted,
but they'll
wander in!

They're wily! You have to wage war, or they'll win.
A gardener must not only wrestle with weeds,
He also must watch over plants' water needs.
He's always on top of the weather reports.
A gardener is almost a wizard of sorts.
He fills WINDOW BOXES with billowing flower
And weaves the WISTERIA into a bower.
He welcomes the WILDFLOWERS while on his walk,
Hears whispering WOLFBANE and WAKE ROBINS talk
And when he's away from the world he creates,
He's ever aware that the WHEELBARROW waits.

A WOODPECKER bird seems to wear a red wig.
A WALKING STICK insect looks much like a twig.
Where are they? Would you call that walking stick big?

**X**ERISCAPE
garden plants
stand up to drought.
They don't use
much water.
They'll do fine without.

**Y**UCCA, with long,
sword-like leaves
likes it dry.
If you want to
xeriscape,
give it a try.

YARROW has flowers that have a flat top.
The yellow kind makes a nice butterfly stop.
What shrubs can form backdrops for any yard's view?
Some people like YAUPON best. What about YEW?

# Z

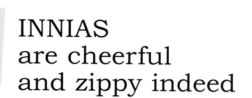

INNIAS
are cheerful
and zippy indeed

And easy to grow from a small pack of seed.
Are summers real hot where you live?
What's your ZONE?
That tells you where plants will be hardy if grown.
Temps drop below zero up north in Zone 3.
Zone 10 is where tropical plants want to be.

Whatever your climate, wherever you live,
Trees, plants and flowers have so much to give.
From faraway castles to good ol' Zone 7,
A garden's like having a small slice of heaven.

Yes, the garden's a place
Very close to God's heart.
And that's why He gave us one
Back at the start.

THE END